LOOK AND SEE

The Bold and the Brave

Leena Lane and Moira Maclean

Adam and Eve

Look! Here is Adam.
Look! Here is Eve.
God wanted them
to look after everything he had made:
the fish of the sea,
the birds of the air,
the animals in the fields,
the animals in the woods.
God made a beautiful world.
He made light and dark,
day and night,
land and sea,
trees and plants,
sun and moon,
stars so bright,
sky above and earth below.
God said: 'It is good.'
He was very pleased.

Which animals can you see?

3

Noah

Look! Here is Noah.
Noah was a friend of God.
God sent a terrible flood.
But Noah was safe.
God told Noah to build a boat.
The boat could float.
Noah put animals in the boat.
Which animals have spots?
Which animals can hop?
It started to rain.
Forty long days and nights it rained.
The earth was covered with water.
At last the rain stopped.
Noah and his animals climbed out.
God put a rainbow in the sky.

Can you name the colours of the rainbow?

5

Abraham and Sarah

Look! Here is Abraham.
Abraham was a friend of God.
God made a promise to Abraham.
'You will have a great family.'
'You will have children
and your children will have children
and they will have children –
more than the stars in the sky
or grains of sand on the beach!'
Abraham believed God.
He waited for a son.
His wife Sarah wanted a child.
But she was now very old.
Abraham believed God's promise.
Many years later, they had a son!
They called him Isaac.
His name means 'laughter'.

Can you see baby Isaac?

7

Isaac and Rebecca

Look! Here is Isaac.
He was Abraham's son.
Abraham wanted him to marry.
He sent a servant to find a wife.
The servant travelled far.
He took ten camels with him.
He stopped by a well.
Rebecca was at the well.
She was fetching water.
She offered the servant a drink
and gave water to the camels.
The servant went to Rebecca's house.
He spoke to Rebecca's father, Bethuel.
He asked Rebecca to be Isaac's wife!
He gave Rebecca fine jewellery.
Later Isaac met Rebecca and loved her.
Rebecca and Isaac were married.

Can you count the camels?

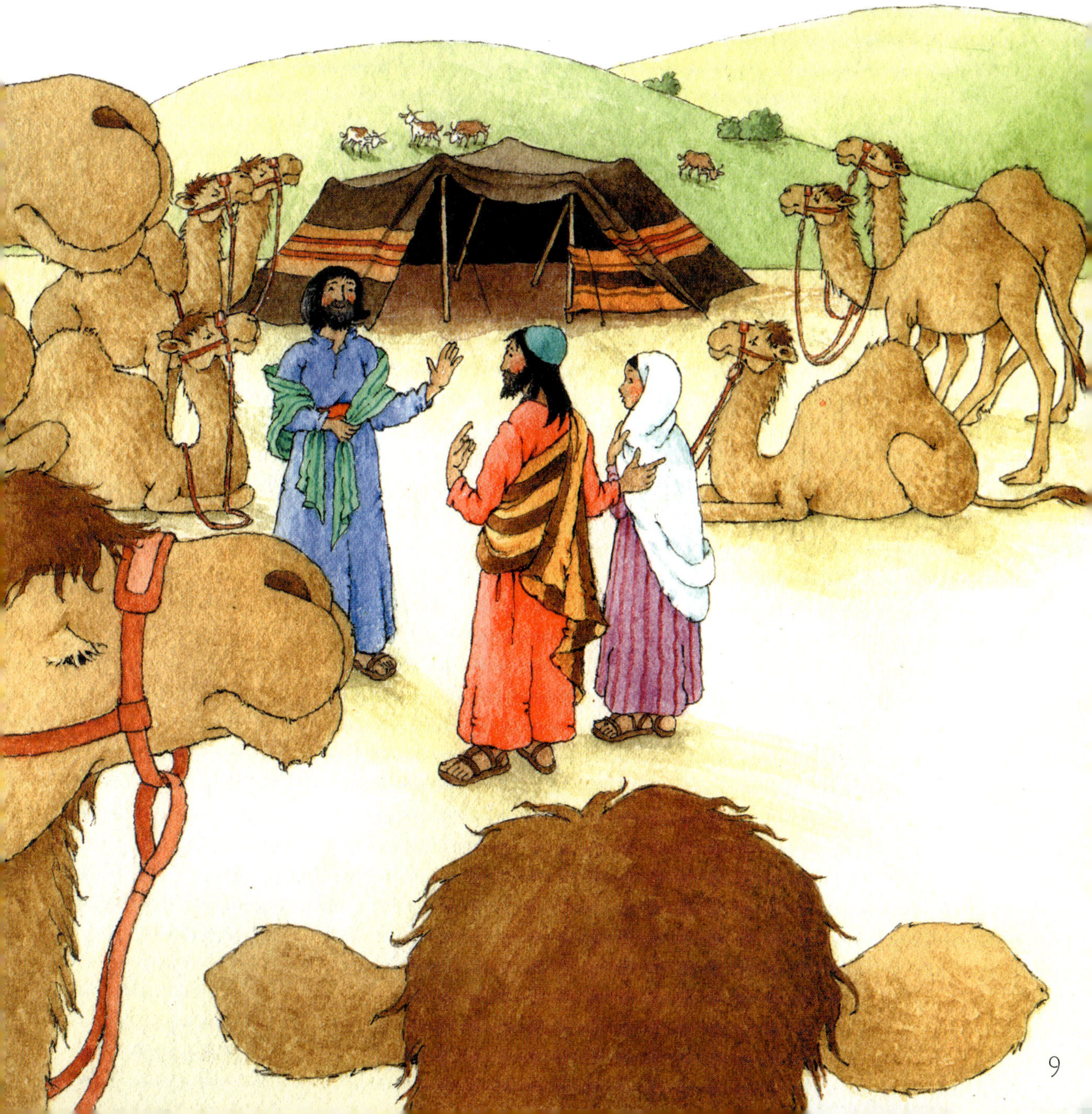

Esau and Jacob

Look! Here is Esau. Look! Here is Jacob.
They were Isaac and Rebecca's sons.
Esau and Jacob were twins.
But they looked very different.
Esau was a hairy man. Jacob had smooth skin.
Esau liked hunting. Jacob liked cooking.
Esau was born first.
He would get his father's blessing.
When Isaac was an old man, he called for Esau.
'Go hunting, then cook me a tasty meal.
Bring it to me. I will give you my blessing.'
Rebecca was listening.
She told Jacob to play a nasty trick.
Jacob pretended to be Esau!
He put goatskin on his arms,
so Isaac thought he was hairy Esau.
Then Jacob got his father's blessing.
Esau was very angry, so Jacob ran away.
It was many years before Esau forgave him.

Who is watching from outside the tent?

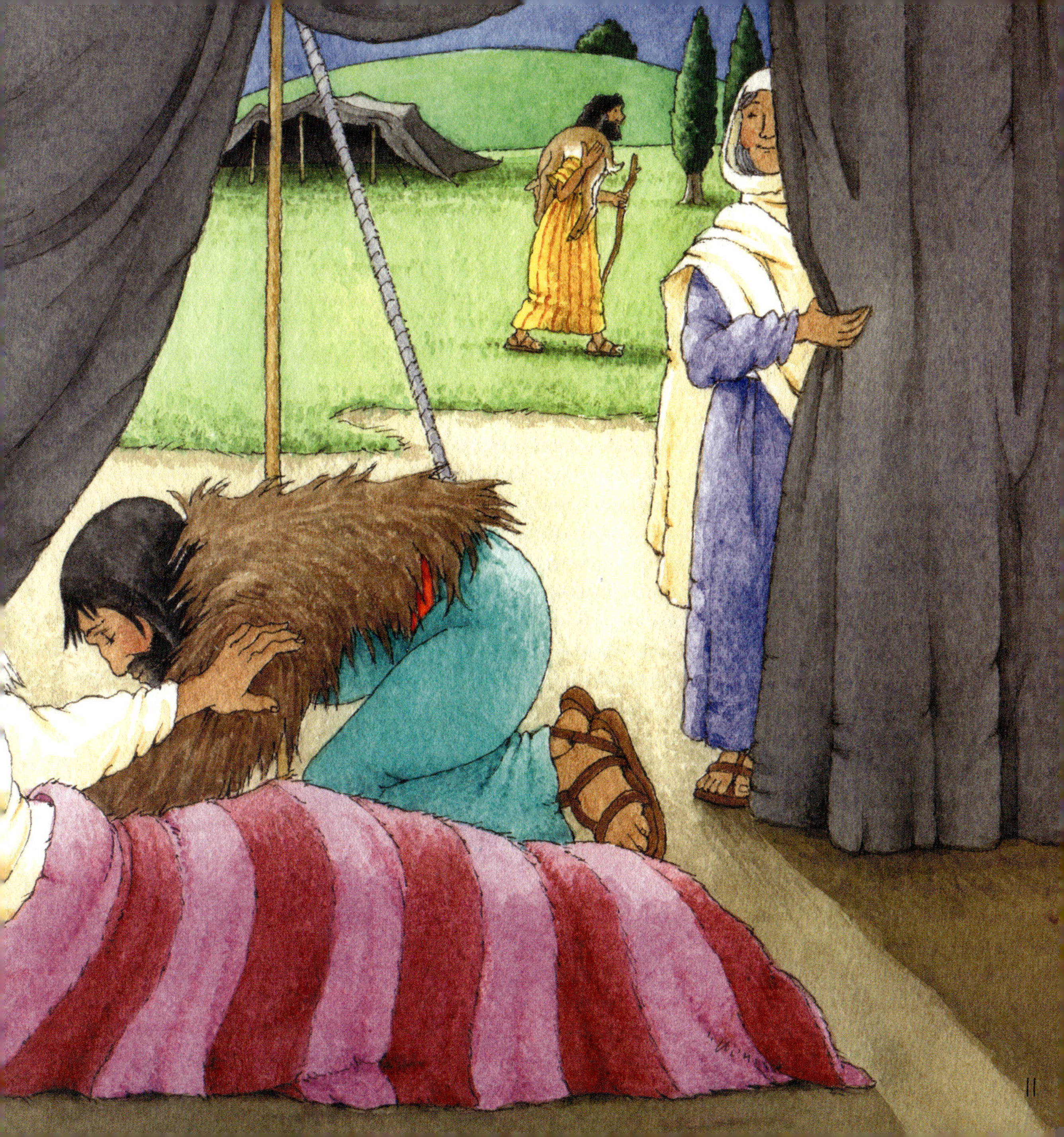

Joseph

Look! Here is Joseph.
Joseph was Jacob's favourite son.
Jacob had twelve sons.
But he loved Joseph most of all.
Jacob gave Joseph a very fine coat.
Joseph was very pleased.
But his brothers were angry.
Then Joseph had two strange dreams.
He boasted to his brothers.
He said he was more important than them.
So the brothers sold him to be a slave!
But God looked after Joseph.
Joseph became a leader in Egypt.
Years later, there was a famine.
Joseph had stored food in Egypt.
His brothers came to him for help.
Joseph forgave his brothers and
the family could be together again at last.

Can you see Joseph's special coat?

13

Moses

Look! Here is Moses.
Moses was born in Egypt, where
the King was very cruel.
He made people his slaves.
Baby Moses was in danger.
His mother hid him from soldiers.
She made a special basket.
She put Moses in it.
She hid the basket near the riverbank.
The princess came to bathe in the river.
She heard a baby crying.
She found the basket.
She found Moses!
Moses' sister Miriam was watching.
She told the princess that her mother could help.
So Moses lived with his mother again.
When he was older he lived in the palace.
Moses grew up to be a great leader.

Can you see the basket in the reeds?

15

Joshua

Look! Here is Joshua.
Joshua was a very brave man.
Joshua was leading God's people into
a wonderful new land.
God was helping them.
Now they were near Jericho.
Jericho had very strong walls.
The people inside were fierce.
There was no way through the city.
What could Joshua do?
God told Joshua what to do.
They marched round the walls for six days.
Seven priests carried trumpets.
On the seventh day,
they marched around the city seven times.
1, 2, 3, 4, 5, 6, 7...
The priests blew their trumpets...
All the people shouted...
The walls of the city crashed to the ground!

Can you count the trumpets?

17

Deborah

Look! Here is Deborah.
Deborah was a very wise woman.
The cruel king was called Jabin.
His army chief was called Sisera.
Deborah wanted to free her people.
Deborah listened to God.
Deborah sent for Barak.
Barak could lead the army.
He would fight against Sisera
with ten thousand men.
But Barak didn't want to go!
So Deborah went with him.
They went to Mount Tabor with their army.
Sisera had nine hundred iron chariots.
Barak had ten thousand men.
They came running down the mountain.
They attacked Sisera's army.
Barak's soldiers won the battle!
Deborah sang praises to God.

Can you see Deborah?

19

Gideon

Look! Here is Gideon.
God wanted Gideon to lead the army.
Gideon knew God was on his side.
He would fight against the Midianites.
They were very cruel.
Gideon gave every soldier two things:
a trumpet and a jar.
There was a burning torch inside the jar.
'Copy me!' said Gideon.
'When I blow my trumpet, blow yours.
Shout: "A sword for the Lord and for Gideon!"'
Gideon went to the Midianites' camp.
It was night time.
Gideon blew his trumpet.
So did all his soldiers.
They all smashed their jars on the ground.
They shouted: 'A sword for the Lord and for Gideon!'
And the enemy all ran away!
God helped Gideon win the battle.

Can you see Gideon's trumpet?

Samson

Look! Here is Samson. Samson was very strong.
Samson could kill a lion with his bare hands!
God made him strong.
Samson had long hair.
If his hair was cut, his strength would go.
But it was a secret.
Delilah wanted to know the secret.
The enemy Philistines paid her to find it out.
Delilah asked Samson many times.
Finally he told her about his hair.
When Samson was asleep,
the Philistines cut off his hair!
They captured Samson.
They threw him into prison.
But Samson's hair started to grow...
The Philistines were meeting in a temple.
Samson was in chains.
He pushed the pillars of the temple.
The temple fell down with a terrible crash!
God gave him strength once more.

Can you see Samson's broken chains?

23

Published in the UK by
The Bible Reading Fellowship
First Floor, Elsfield Hall, 15-17 Elsfield Way, Oxford OX2 8FG

ISBN 1 84101 410 9

First edition 2005

Copyright © 2005 AD Publishing Services Ltd
1 Churchgates, The Wilderness, Berkhamsted, Herts HP4 2UB
Text copyright © 2005 AD Publishing Services Ltd, Leena Lane
Illustrations copyright © 2005 Moira Maclean

Editorial Director Annette Reynolds
Art Director Gerald Rogers
Pre-production Krystyna Hewitt
Production John Laister

British Library Cataloguing in Publication Data.
A catalogue record for this book is available from the British Library.

Printed and bound in Singapore